2-18-57

DATE DUE

★

FORTY GOSPEL HYMN STORIES

★

FORTY GOSPEL HYMN STORIES

BY

GEORGE W. SANVILLE

PUBLISHED BY

THE RODEHEAVER-HALL MACK CO.

WINONA LAKE, INDIANA

Printed in U. S. A., 1945

TO MY WIFE . . .

HARRIET S. SANVILLE

whose companionship brought to my life
a finer melody. Whatever success I have
enjoyed has come to me through her
helpful inspiration and encouragement.

F O R E W O R D

One who writes a book should know the material about which he writes. If it is a biography, he should live with the people of whom he writes.

The author of this book knows his material and has lived with the gospel songs and hymns and their writers.

George W. Sanville has had as his close personal friends more of the authors of gospel songs and hymns than any living man. Only through this friendship could one get the intimate personal stories that are so valuable and should be preserved.

When I first met him years ago I wanted him in our business. He was the manager of a successful publishing company. To get him I had to buy the other company, and it has been one of my best investments, both in business and friendship. He has been a most loyal and faithful friend and an efficient associate through the years.

We have had to urge him to take the time to write the stories, and now he shares with you these rich experiences of many years, with the hope that by knowing the authors better, you will love the hymns more. By loving them more you will sing them better, bringing greater joy to you and greater blessing to the multitudes who need the message of the gospel in song.

HOMER RODEHEAVER.

Winona Lake, Ind.

P R E F A C E

Forty years' association with authors and composers of gospel hymns, many of them friends or co-workers, gave me the rare opportunity to secure authentic stories of the experiences which gave birth to many of our gospel hymns.

I have selected forty of these stories, covering a wide variety of spiritual experiences. They are told with direct simplicity, as are all fundamental truths. Their personal testimony confirms the transformation wrought in the lives by the Gospel, ringing with the triumphant note of spiritual victory. Thus the gospel hymns make a unique and invaluable contribution to the preaching of the Word.

The story of their origin is a great stimulus to faith, for they are filled with the realization, "Surely God was in this place."

The gospel hymns' forthright testimony of God's transforming power is as fresh as water from the mountain spring, and as refreshing.

May these simple, inspiring stories make the service of the church more enjoyable and of lasting benefit in helping Christians to a better understanding of our gospel hymns.

INDEX

O THAT WILL BE GLORY
(The Glory Song)

"Heaven aflame in the face of a man" is the description given of Ed Card, "Old Glory Face," superintendent of the Sunshine Rescue Mission, St. Louis, Mo. Mr. Charles H. Gabriel says the Glory Song was inspired by the slogan which this man used during the Rescue Mission meetings. His one and only safety valve for the pent-up enthusiasm generated in him during the service was his frequent utterance of "Glory!" He praised God, not with many words, but one word many times repeated.

Though he used but this one word, he played with it as a virtuoso with one string on his violin. He sang his song of praise to God with a charm and earnestness that carried a conviction of holy reverence to all who heard.

At the time of prayer he led praying souls to another Jacob's ladder, a vision with the angels of heaven ascending and descending to ministries of blessing. In prayer he drew men nearer to the God he served. His prayer invariably ended with, "And that will be glory for me."

"Old Glory Face" now sings his song in the Glory Land. He lived here long enough to sing this Glory Song which he inspired. He came to know his life before men had been a good testimony of the saving grace of the Lord Jesus Christ.

The Glory Song literally burst into popularity. It has been sung around the world in many dialects and languages. Millions of copies have been printed, and 43 years of use attest to the deserved popularity of this gospel song.

The author, Charles H. Gabriel, has been called the Prince of Gospel Song Writers. He has given the world a host of songs that will live. He has left us, but the touch of a vanished hand, and the sound of a voice that is still, lives on through his great ministry in song.

"The glory of the Lord shone round about Him."

O THAT WILL BE GLORY

C. H. G.

Words and music

CHAS. H. GABRIEL

1. When all my la-bors and tri-als are o'er, And I am safe on that
2. When, by the gift of His in-fi-nite grace, I am ac-cord-ed in
3. Friends will be there I have loved long a-go; Joy like a riv-er a-

beau-ti-ful shore, Just to be near the dear Lord I a-dore,
heav-en a place, Just to be there and to look on His face,
round me will flow; Yet, just a smile from my Sav-ior, I know,

rit.

CHORUS. *Faster.*

Will thro' the a-ges be glo-ry for me.... O that will be
O................ that will

glo-ry for me, Glo-ry for me, glo-ry for me; When by His grace
be glo-ry for me, glo-ry for me, glo-ry for me;............

rit.

I shall look on His face, That will be glo-ry, be glo-ry for me.

SUNRISE

"Do not feel sorry for me, brethren," said the Methodist minister to his fellow pastors as he was accepting retired relationship at the Wilmington, Del., conference. "The end of my days here is not sunset for me, but sunrise! You see the end of this life is not death but resurrection unto eternal life; not crying but rejoicing; not a funeral but a festival. If God should call me home, it would be but the beginning of life eternal. You have the wrong emphasis when you speak of my having reached the sunset time of life. I am walking steadily into the sunrise of tomorrow."

I was leading the congregational singing at the conference and the event made a deep impression on me. He accepted his retired relationship as a crowning reward of faithful service. His testimony came from a warm heart and glowed with enthusiastic appreciation of his journey onward and upward. He gave evidence of the useful Christian growing into full flower of life. He seemed to feel that whatever his native endowments had been, they had been ripening under God's control. He was positive that the splendid days of his ministry were the promise that the best was yet to be.

Rev. Wm. C. Poole, a member of the conference, caught the inspiration of that warm-hearted, thankful testimony, and crystallized it in a poetic gem — Sunrise.

B. D. Ackley furnishes an ideal musical vehicle for the words.

> "When I shall come to the end of my way,
> When I shall rest at the close of life's day,
> When 'Welcome home' I shall hear Jesus say,
> O! that will be sunrise for me."

SUNRISE

W. C. Poole

B. D. Ackley

SOLO

1. When I shall come to the end of my way, When I shall rest at the
2. When in His beau-ty I see the great King, Join with the ran-somed His
3. When life is o - ver and day-light is passed, In heav-en's har - bor my

close of life's day, When "Wel-come home" I shall hear Je - sus say, O
prais - es to sing, When I shall join them my trib - utes to bring, O
an - chor is cast, When I see Je - sus my Sav - ior at last, O

CHORUS

that will be sun-rise for me. . . . . Sun-rise to-mor-row, sun-rise to-

mor-row, Sun-rise in glo - ry is wait-ing for me; Sun-rise to-mor-row,

sun-rise to-mor-row, Sun-rise with Je - sus for e - ter - ni - ty.

IN THE GARDEN

"One day in March, 1912, I was seated in the dark-room, where I kept my photographic equipment, and organ. I drew my Bible toward me; it opened at my favorite chapter, John XX — whether by chance or inspiration let each reader decide. That meeting of Jesus and Mary had lost none of its power to charm.

"As I read it that day, I seemed to be part of the scene. I became a silent witness to that dramatic moment in Mary's life, when she knelt before her Lord, and cried, 'Rabboni!'

"My hands were resting on the Bible while I stared at the light blue wall. As the light faded I seemed to be standing at the entrance of a garden, looking down a gently winding path, shaded by olive branches. A woman in white, with head bowed, hand clasping her throat, as if to choke back her sobs, walked slowly into the shadows. It was Mary. As she came to the tomb, upon which she placed her hand, she bent over to look in, and hurried away.

"John, in flowing robe, appeared, looking at the tomb; then came Peter, who entered the tomb, followed slowly by John.

"As they departed, Mary reappeared, leaning her head upon her arm at the tomb, she wept. Turning herself, she saw Jesus standing, so did I. I knew it was He. She knelt before Him, with arms outstretched and looking into His face cried 'Rabboni!'

"I awakened in full light, gripping the Bible, with muscles tense and nerves vibrating. Under the inspiration of this vision I wrote as quickly as the words could be formed the poem exactly as it has since appeared. That same evening I wrote the music."

Thus writes C. Austin Miles of the remarkable experience which has given us "In the Garden."

IN THE GARDEN

C. A. M.

C. Austin Miles

1. I come to the gar-den a - lone, While the dew is still on the ros - es; And the voice I hear, Fall-ing on my ear; The Son of God dis - clos - es.

2. He speaks, and the sound of His voice Is so sweet the birds hush their sing - ing, And the mel - o - dy That He gave to me, With - in my heart is ring - ing.

3. I'd stay in the gar-den with Him Tho' the night a-round me be fall - ing, But He bids me go; Thro' the voice of woe, His voice to me is call - ing.

Chorus

And He walks with me, and He talks with me, And He tells me I am His own, And the joy we share as we tar - ry there, None other has ev - er known.

THE OLD RUGGED CROSS

The center and core of evangelical Christian faith is the Cross. The truth of redemption is the meaning of the Cross. The flowing stream of salvation is the distilled essence of divine grace and love, symbolized by the Cross.

"I was praying for a full understanding of the cross, and its plan in Christianity," said Reverend George Bennard. "I read and studied and prayed. I saw Christ and the Cross inseparably. The Christ of the Cross became more than a symbol. The scene pictured a method, outlined a process, and revealed the consummation of spiritual experience. It was like seeing John 3:16 leave the printed page, take form, and act out the meaning of redemption. While watching this scene with my mind's eye, the theme of the song came to me, and with it the melody; but only the words of the theme, 'The Old Rugged Cross,' came. An inner voice seemed to say, 'Wait'!

"I was holding evangelistic meetings in Michigan, but could not continue with the poem. After a series of meetings in New York state, the following week, I tried again to compose the poem, but could not. It was only after I had completed the New York meeting, and returned to Michigan for further evangelistic work, that the flood-gates were loosed.

"Many experiences of the redeeming grace of God through our Lord Jesus Christ during those meetings had broken down all barriers. I was enabled to complete the poem with facility and dispatch. A friend aided in putting it into manuscript form. Charles H. Gabriel, to whom the manuscript was sent, returned it with a prophetic statement: 'You will hear from this song.' Likewise, when I strummed my guitar and sang it to Reverend and Mrs. Bostwick, upon my return to Michigan, they felt as had Mr. Gabriel, for they said: 'God has given you a song that will never die. It has moved us as no other song ever has moved us.' "

The unprecedented acceptance of "The Old Rugged Cross" justifies these statements. Around the world, on radio, where it has been the most used gospel song, and in multitudinous religious meetings, this arrow of the gospel, shafted with music, has shot God's truth home to the hearts of men. It is the epitome of the gospel in song; it is in the world of gospel song what John 3:16 is in gospel doctrine — the heart of it.

THE OLD RUGGED CROSS

Rev. George Bennard   Rev. George Bennard

1. On a hill far a-way stood an old rug-ged cross, The em-blem of
2. Oh, the old rug-ged cross, so de-spised by the world, Has a wondrous at-
3. In the old rug-ged cross, stained with blood so di-vine, A won - drous
4. To the old rug-ged cross I will ev - er be true, Its shame and re-

suf-f'ring and shame; And I love that old cross where the dear-est and best
trac-tion for me; For the dear Lamb of God left His glo - ry a-bove
beau - ty I see; For 'twas on that old cross Je - sus suf-fered and died
proach gladly bear; Then He'll call me some day to my home far a - way,

For a world of lost sin-ners was slain.   So I'll cher-ish the old rug-ged
To   bear it to dark Cal - va - ry.
To   par-don and sanc-ti - fy me.
Where His glo-ry for - ev - er I'll share.   cross, the

CHORUS

cross, ... Till my tro-phies at last I lay down; I will cling to the
old rug-ged cross,

old rug-ged cross, ... And ex-change it some day for a crown.
cross,   the old rug - ged cross,

GOOD-NIGHT AND GOOD-MORNING

Ploughing the soul with the sorrow of a great loss often turns into the furrow some nuggets of gold. When Mrs. Lizzie DeArmond lost one of her lovely daughters she was deeply stricken. Her struggle to understand the great question, "Why?" revealed a depth of character that has given us the comforting message of "Good-night and Good-morning." Like so many gospel hymns, it has come to us because someone had to say "good-bye" to a loved one.

Mrs. DeArmond said to me, "Mr. Sanville, when God called my girl to live with Him, I felt I could not spare her, and it left an ache in my heart that was difficult to bear. The ever-present, persistent question, 'Why should my girl be taken?' became the overwhelming burden of my waking moments. Why should it be my child?

"After several months of wrestling with this question, my health was affected and my faith clouded. Then one night, while I was pacing up and down on my lawn, there came to me the words as if spoken from the sky: 'We Christians do not sorrow without hope. We do have to say good-bye to our loved ones here, but we have that glorious hope of good-morning over there.'

"The message brought surcease from my sorrow, comfort for my heart, and stimulus to my faith. I hastened to my room where the poem took form. God gave me a song that has been a blessing in my life, as it will be to others who sorrow for loved ones."

Homer Rodeheaver wrote the musical score for this lovely poem. The evident fine balance between music and poem has brought forth a song of peace and comfort to all who must say "Good-bye" to loved ones.

"Let not your heart be troubled; . . . where I am, there ye shall be also."

GOOD-NIGHT AND GOOD-MORNING

Lizzie DeArmond
Homer A. Rodeheaver

1. When comes to the wea-ry a bless-ed re-lease, When upward we
2. When fad-eth the day and dark shadows draw nigh, With Christ close at
3. When home-lights we see shin-ing bright-ly a-bove, Where we shall be

pass to His kingdom of peace, When free from the woes that on earth we must bear,
hand, it is not death to die; He'll wipe ev-'ry tear, roll a-way ev-'ry care;
soon, thro' His wonderful love, We'll praise Him who called us His heaven to share,

CHORUS.

We'll say "good-night," here, but "good-morning" up there.
We'll say "good-night," here, but "good-morning" up there. Good morning up there where
We'll say "good-night," here, but "good-morning" up there.

Christ is the Light, Good-morning up there where cometh no night; When we step from this

earth to God's heaven so fair, We'll say "good-night" here, but "good-morning" up there.

BRIGHTEN THE CORNER

This is a symphony of the common-place. A symphony whose themes and variations are the common household duties. This lilting Gospel song of good advice was born of frustration.

Mrs. Ina Duley Ogdon, who would have been satisfied to have had an audience of thousands on the Chautauqua circuits, actually reached many millions because the denial of her great ambition opened the door into a far wider field. Her well-planned and well-prepared-for career was abandoned through necessity. Her cherished ambition was defeated by the invalidism of her father. Mrs. Ogdon, who had hoped to reach the multitudes of Chautauqua circuits, had to compromise with an audience of one in the seclusion of a home.

The difficulty of reconciling herself to the loss of a great ambition, added to the duties which accompany the care of an invalid father, seemed almost unbearable. The transition from resentment to quiet acceptance was rapid. "Do not wait until some deed of greatness you may do — do not wait to shed your light afar" — she was thinking of a Chautauqua career. Then under the performance of her household duties she emerged, bit by bit, into a state of glad and enthusiastic delight in her household tasks. Her faithful and glad performance of those duties sang a song in her heart. She brought it out and gave it voice in this joyous song:

"To the many duties ever near you now be true" — she was thinking of dish-washing, sweeping, and the commonplace household duties — "Brighten the corner where you are."

This homespun, lilting lyric, with its good advice, shows again how God moves in a mysterious way His wonders to perform.

Mrs. Ogdon, who might have spoken to thousands via Chautauqua, by providential intervention reached millions. More than twenty-five million reproductions of "Brighten the Corner" have been made in hymn books, radio transcriptions, phonograph records and moving pictures. Greater than any early dream was the working out of her early disappointment.

Charles H. Gabriel made the musical setting that has added effectiveness to the song. Homer Rodeheaver's use of the song as a theme song has been responsible for its wide hearing.

BRIGHTEN THE CORNER

INA DULEY OGDON

CHAS. H. GABRIEL

1. Do not wait un-til some deed of great-ness you may do, Do not wait to shed your light a-far, To the man-y du-ties ev-er near you now be true, Bright-en the cor-ner where you are.

2. Just a-bove are cloud-ed skies that you may help to clear, Let not nar-row self your way de-bar, Tho' in-to one heart a-lone may fall your song of cheer, Bright-en the cor-ner where you are.

3. Here for all your tal-ent you may sure-ly find a need, Here re-flect the Bright and Morning Star, E-ven from your humble hand the bread of life may feed, Bright-en the cor-ner where you are.

REFRAIN

Bright-en the cor-ner where you are! Bright-en the cor-ner where you are! Some one far from har-bor you may guide a-cross the bar, Bright-en the cor-ner where you are.

Shine for Je-sus where you are!

GOD'S TOMORROW

" 'God's tomorrow! God's tomorrow!' kept ringing in my mind during my Rally Day speech on another subject," writes Rev. A. H. Ackley. "Along with the song came the vision of the words like a moving picture, flashing with increasingly rapid projection on the screen of my mind. The sound stepped up its tempo, and the rapidity of the word images increased until they obliterated all thought of the prepared address. The persistence of the idea, 'God's tomorrow,' obsessed my thought so that it crowded out all else, and I told my Rally Day audience of God's tomorrow.

"The words 'God's tomorrow' had appeared as the caption of a Rally Day program; they had caught my eye while waiting for the service to begin. Immediately they struck me as a suggestive and unusual title for a gospel song.

"Quietly leaving the platform, I went to the manse next door. The beautiful words, 'God's tomorrow,' were ringing like sweet bells in my heart. I sat down at the piano and the melody was born immediately. I had no sooner reached the chorus than the words came spontaneously:

> God's tomorrow, God's tomorrow!
> Every cloud will pass away,
> At the dawning of that day.
> God's tomorrow, no more sorrow!
> For I know that God's tomorrow
> Will be better than today.

"So when I hastened back to the Rally Day platform to speak, my mind was full of 'God's tomorrow.' I was impelled to abandon the announced address of the program and speak on 'God's tomorrow.' I simply used it as a text for a talk on Heaven.

"I finished by telling about writing the new hymn. I had them sing the chorus as a climax to the address. How they did sing it!"

GOD'S TOMORROW

A. H. A.

A. H. Ackley

1. God's tomorrow is a day of gladness, And its joys shall nev-er fade;
2. God's tomorrow is a day of greeting: We shall see the Savior's face;
3. God's tomorrow is a day of glo-ry: We shall wear the crown of life;

No more weeping, no more sense of sad-ness, No more foes to make a-fraid.
And our longing hearts a-wait the meeting In that ho-ly, hap-py place.
Sing thro' countless years love's old, old story, Free for-ev-er from all strife.

REFRAIN.

God's to-mor-row, God's to-mor-row, Ev-'ry cloud will pass a-way
At the dawning of that day; God's to-mor-row, No more sor-row,
For I know that God's to-mor-row Will be bet-ter than to-day!

LIVING FOR JESUS

"Write me a poem for this music," wrote C. Harold Lowden to T. O. Chisholm. "I need the right words for this melody. After much thought and earnest prayer, God has directed me to you." Mr. Chisholm heard the plea and responded in a very short time. The wedding of poem and music was a happy one, for it was immediately evident that a harmonious union had been effected.

The music had been written in 1915 for a Children's Day service. The words for the original song had all the ephemeral characteristics of a dated service; but there was a general urge to save the music by finding a suitable poem. So the music was filed away. Two years later, while searching for material for a new hymn collection, Mr. Lowden was impressed with the beauty of the melody. The tempo and rhythm suggested the words, "Living for Jesus." This then was the title sent with music to Mr. Chisholm for a poem of consecration. The thrilling outcome of that request is the completed song. In addition to translation in fifteen languages and inclusion in a score of hymn books, more than a million copies were issued.

Here is a duality of inspiration — Mr. Lowden for title, refrain, and music; Mr. Chisholm for the poem. God breathed and two men moved. One wrote a melody, another penned a poem.

LIVING FOR JESUS

T. O. Chisholm

C. Harold Lowden

Not fast

1. Liv-ing for Je-sus a life that is true, Striving to please Him in all that I do,
2. Liv-ing for Je-sus who died in my place, Bearing on Calv'ry my sin and disgrace,
3. Liv-ing for Je-sus wher-ev-er I am, Do-ing each du-ty in His Ho-ly Name,
4. Living for Jesus thro' earth's little while, My dearest treasure, the light of His smile,

Yielding allegiance, glad-hearted and free, This is the pathway of blessing for me.
Such love constrains me to answer His call, Follow His leading and give Him my all.
Will-ing to suf-fer af-flic-tion or loss, Deeming each trial a part of my cross.
Seek-ing the lost ones He died to redeem, Bringing the weary to find rest in Him.

Chorus. Unison. A little slower.

O Je-sus, Lord and Savior, I give my-self to Thee; For Thou, in Thy a-
tonement, Didst give Thyself for me; I own no oth-er Mas-ter, My
heart shall be Thy throne, My life I give, henceforth to live, O Christ, for Thee alone.

*Melody in lower notes. A two-part effect may be had by having the men sing the melody, the women taking the middle notes.

THEN JESUS CAME

What a difference the presence of Jesus makes! The loneliness, sadness, and despair of Mary and Martha disappeared when Jesus came.

Dr. Harry Rimmer described the scene in the home of the dead Lazarus with keen understanding. The deeply felt loss of the sisters, the shadow which death casts across the threshold by visitation, the ache of separation, all these he enumerated, but after a brief silent pause he electrified his audience with the triumphant shout: "Then Jesus came; that changed everything!"

Homer Rodeheaver was one of those sharply startled, but deeply impressed by the words, "Then Jesus came; that changed everything!" He recognized in it an idea for a song. When he came into our office in Philadelphia, Dr. Oswald Smith happened to be there, so he, Mr. Rodeheaver and Mr. Ackley discussed what a beautiful song could be made from the theme, "Then Jesus Came." Dr. Smith returned to his room at the China Inland Mission headquarters, in Philadelphia, filled with the idea. He worked zealously, completing the poem that day. He gave the lyric to Mr. Rodeheaver, who composed the musical setting. The song has had instant success.

The presentation of the song as a five-part drama is Mr. Rodeheaver's unique contribution. Each verse is dramatized and then sung. The effect is cumulative and moves to a stirring climax. It has leaped into high popularity. More requests are received for this song than any other we have published.

We believe that God had His own way in producing the song; first, through the masterly preaching of Dr. Rimmer, the poem by Dr. Oswald J. Smith, the music by Mr. Homer Rodeheaver, and its unique dramatic presentation.

THEN JESUS CAME

OSWALD J. SMITH   HOMER RODEHEAVER

1. One sat a-lone be-side the high-way beg-ging,   His eyes were blind, the
2. From home and friends the e-vil spir-its drove him,   A-mong the tombs he
3. Un-clean! un-clean! the lep-er cried in tor-ment,   The deaf, the dumb, in
4. So men to-day have found the Sav-iour a-ble,   They could not con-quer

light he could not see; He clutched his rags and shivered in the shad-ows, Then Je-sus
dwelt in mis-er-y;   He cut him-self as demon pow'rs possessed him, Then Jesus
helplessness stood near; The fev-er raged, disease had gripped its victim, Then Je-sus
pas-sion, lust and sin; Their broken hearts had left them sad and lonely, Then Je-sus

REFRAIN

came and bade his dark-ness flee.
came and set the cap-tive free.
came and cast out ev-'ry fear.
came and dwelt Himself with-in.

When Je-sus comes the tempter's pow'r is

bro-ken; When Je-sus comes the tears are wiped a-way. He takes the

gloom and fills the life with glory, For all is changed when Jesus comes to stay.

LET JESUS COME INTO YOUR HEART

An altar service, the kneeling penitent, the praying intercessors, helping a seeking soul to find Christ, mark the unforgettable scene when "Let Jesus Come Into Your Heart" was born.

Here is drama, deeply-moving, and soul-stirring. The pen of no playwright can adorn its sheer beauty. No stage scenery can rival its perfect setting. No acting can better personalize the realism of the truth here depicted in living characters. It is God dealing with the human soul.

At the Sunday morning service, Mountain Lake Park, Maryland, camp meeting, the minister preached with apostolic fervor. His zeal for saving souls charged his message with spiritual power. His handling of his theme, "Repentance," brought many to the altar. One was a woman of culture and refinement. As she knelt and prayed, she gave evidence of the inner struggle taking place. She wanted to do something—to give, not receive. Mrs. C. H. Morris quietly joined her at the altar, put her arm around her, and prayed with her. Mrs. Morris said, "Just now your doubting give o'er." Dr. H. L. Gilmour, song leader of the camp meeting, added another phrase, "Just now reject Him no more." L. H. Baker, the preacher of the sermon, earnestly importuned, "Just now throw open the door." Mrs. Morris made the last appeal, "Let Jesus Come Into Your Heart."

Thus was born that morning the chorus of this justly famous song. Simultaneously, and more important, a soul was born into the Kingdom. Mrs. Morris completed the hymn before the close of the camp meeting. This hymn is unique in the contribution made by the participators, and stands as a great testimony to the transforming power of the Holy Spirit through the preached Word.

[28]

LET JESUS COME INTO YOUR HEART

C. H. M.

Mrs. C. H. MORRIS

1. If you are tired of the load of your sin, Let Je - sus come
2. If 'tis for pu - ri - ty now that you sigh, Let Je - sus come
3. If there's a tem - pest your voice can - not still, Let Je - sus come
4. If you would join the glad songs of the blest, Let Je - sus come

in - to your heart; If you de - sire a new life to be - gin,
in - to your heart; Fountains for cleans-ing are flow-ing near by,
in - to your heart; If there's a void this world nev - er can fill,
in - to your heart; If you would en - ter the man-sions of rest,

CHORUS

Let Je - sus come in - to your heart. Just now, your

doubt-ings give o'er; Just now, re - ject Him no more; Just now, throw

o - pen the door; Let Je - sus come in - to your heart.

GOD UNDERSTANDS

How "nearer than breathing . . . and closer than hands and feet" is the help of God in the trying time of deep disaster! How varied the agencies by which He ministers His grace to the stricken! In this case it was a blood-brother, and a minister of the Gospel of His love, that God used to comfort and strengthen the bereaved.

Mrs. Clifford Bicker, sister of the writer of this poem, was the wife of Rev. Clifford Bicker, missionaries with Kingdom work in Peru, South America. During their time in Peru, two children were born to them. As the time of their furlough home approached, their keen anticipation of the trip grew.

Shortly before the sailing time, Mr. Bicker was instantly killed in an automobile accident. Mrs. Bicker buried his body in Peru and set sail with her two little fatherless children for the long, bleak journey home. She was a widow at 26.

Dr. Oswald J. Smith desired that his sister should make the journey home in an atmosphere of hope. He wrote for her this lovely poem, "God Understands." She received it before she sailed for home. It was a great comfort to her. She rested her heart upon its truth, tested and was refreshed by the living water, "God is a very present help in time of trouble," for "God understands and cares."

B. D. Ackley, when he wrote the music for the poem, matched the direct-simplicity of its poetic truth by a strongly beautiful musical setting for a Gospel hymn. During its composition this melody sounded through the walls of my office, which adjoined his. From the first hearing it had a haunting effect upon me. I found myself humming it over and over. When I started my commuting trip to my Ocean City home, the melody rang through my head the entire trip.

The wedding of words and music is splendidly done. Again we have the right musical vehicle to carry home to the heart God's comfort.

"God looketh on the heart."

GOD UNDERSTANDS

OSWALD J. SMITH

B. D. ACKLEY

Slowly, with expression

1. God un - der-stands your sor - row, He sees the fall - ing tear,
2. God un - der-stands your heart-ache, He knows the bit - ter pain;
3. God un - der-stands your weak-ness, He knows the tempt - er's pow'r;

And whispers, "I am with thee," Then fal - ter not, nor fear.
O, trust Him in the dark - ness, You can - not trust in vain.
And He will walk be - side you How - ev - er dark the hour.

CHORUS

He un - der-stands your long - ing, Your deepest grief He shares;

Then let Him bear your bur - den, He un - der-stands, and cares.

SINCE JESUS CAME INTO MY HEART

"What a wonderful change in my life has been wrought
Since Jesus came into my heart,"

runs the testimony of a new convert. The greatest preaching in the world is personal testimony of the experience of salvation. It is greater than promise or prophecy; it is the beginning of life eternal. This first-hand dealing with God has in it the seed of growth which flowers forth into the full statured Christian life.

This kind of spiritual experience is not only a personal possession but starts a relationship with God that recreates life into newness of effort, energy, and destiny.

All this is beautifully set forth in the poem of R. H. McDaniel. Mark the progression of the convert's experience: "Wonderful change; ceased wandering and going astray; possessed of a hope; light in the valley of death;" and "I shall go there to dwell in that city, I know."

Small wonder it was the instrument used by the Holy Spirit in the conversion of Policeman Fowler during the Billy Sunday, Philadelphia, meeting. What the apostolic preaching of the great evangelist failed to do, this song of *personal testimony* did — brought about Fowler's conversion. More than a hundred policemen were led to Christ because of the change wrought in the life of one man by this song.

Charles H. Gabriel wrote the music, and with Homer Rodeheaver introduced it from leaflet at the Philadelphia meetings. It became necessary to print thousands of single copies for use, so great was the spiritual appetite for this fine personal testimony.

It is the greatest of preaching made available to all through the medium of gospel song.

"Behold, I make all things new."

SINCE JESUS CAME INTO MY HEART

R. H. McDaniel

Chas. H. Gabriel

1. What a won - der - ful change in my life has been wrought Since Je-sus came
2. I have ceased from my wand'ring and go - ing a - stray, Since Je-sus came
3. I'm possessed of a hope that is stead - fast and sure, Since Je-sus came
4. There's a light in the val - ley of death now for me, Since Je-sus came
5. I shall go there to dwell in that cit - y I know, Since Je-sus came

in - to my heart; I have light in my soul for which long I had sought,
in - to my heart; And my sins which were ma-ny are all washed a - way,
in - to my heart; And no dark clouds of doubt now my path-way ob-scure,
in - to my heart; And the gates of the cit - y be - yond I can see,
in - to my heart; And I'm hap - py, so hap - py, as on - ward I go,

CHORUS

Since Je - sus came in - to my heart. Since Je - sus came in - to my
Since Je - sus came in, came

heart, Since Je-sus came in-to my heart; Floods of joy o'er my
in - to my heart, Since Je-sus came in, came in - to my heart;

soul like the sea - bil-lows roll, Since Je - sus came in - to my heart.

HE LIVES!

"He lives! I tell you, He is not dead, but lives here and now! Jesus Christ is more alive today than ever before. I can prove it by my own experience, as well as the testimony of countless thousands," answered Rev. A. H. Ackley to a young Jew. This man had attended the evening evangelistic service for five or six successive nights. This night he remained at the close of the service for further light on a statement about the divine presence of Jesus made in that sermon. He had previously demonstrated his increased interest by steady attendance, but now was concerned by what he must do if what the minister so positively stated was true. So Mr. Ackley endeavored to persuade him to accept Christ, laying emphasis upon that first step of surrendering his life to God in acceptance of Jesus Christ as his Saviour and Lord. His question startled Mr. Ackley.

"Why," asked he, "should I worship a dead Jew?" Mr. Ackley's forthright, emphatic answer, together with his subsequent triumphant effort to win the man for Christ, flowered forth into song and crystallized into a convincing sermon on "He Lives!" His keenly alert mind was sensitive to suggestions for sermons, and sermons in song. In his re-reading of the resurrection stories of the Gospels, the words "He is risen" struck him with new meaning. From the thrill within his own soul he wrote the convincing song — "He Lives!" The scriptural evidence, his own heart, and the testimony of history matched the glorious experience of an innumerable cloud of witnesses that "He lives," so he sat down at the piano and voiced that conclusion in song. He says, "The thought of His ever-living presence brought the music promptly and easily. The words followed immediately.

> "He lives! He lives! Christ Jesus lives today,
> He walks with me, and talks with me
> Along life's narrow way.
> He lives! He lives! Salvation to impart;
> You ask me how I know He lives —
> He lives within my heart!"

HE LIVES!

A. H. A.

Rev. A. H. Ackley

1. I serve a ris-en Sav-iour, He's in the world to-day; I know that He is liv-ing, what-
2. In all the world a-round me I see His lov-ing care, And tho' my heart grows weary I
3. Rejoice, rejoice, O Chris-tian, lift up your voice and sing E-ter-nal hal-le-lu-jahs to

ev-er men may say; I see His hand of mer-cy, I hear His voice of cheer, And
nev-er will de-spair; I know that He is lead-ing, thro' all the storm-y blast, The
Je-sus Christ the King! The Hope of all who seek Him, the Help of all who find, None

REFRAIN *Spirited*

just the time I need Him He's al-ways near. He lives, He lives, Christ Jesus lives to-
day of His ap-pear-ing will come at last. He lives, He lives,
oth-er is so lov-ing, so good and kind.

day! He walks with me and talks with me along life's narrow way. He lives, He lives, sal-
He lives, He lives,

rit. ff

va-tion to im-part! You ask me how I know He lives? He lives with-in my heart.

SOME DAY THE SILVER CORD WILL BREAK
(Saved by Grace)

"I cannot see the sunset, but some day I shall see my Saviour face to face," exclaimed Fanny Crosby. This was her reply to Dr. L. W. Munhall's glowing description of the sunset, after a service of the Poughkeepsie camp meeting. Dr. Munhall, the great Methodist layman evangelist, was my traveling companion motoring from the Ocean Grove, N. J., camp meeting when he told me the experience which gave birth to this hymn.

Seated on the hotel porch, he painted with colorful adjective and skillful touch to the blind Fanny Crosby, the deepening glory of the changing sunset. He depicted the roseate hues and shafting lights with accurate phrase, hoping to have her see it, even as he saw it; but she was seeing beyond the brilliance of the sunset, and gave the world this lovely message in song. Hers was not more sight, but finer seeing—spiritual insight:

> Some day when fades the golden sun
> Beneath the rosy-tinted west,
> My blessed Lord shall say, "Well done,"
> And I shall enter into rest.
> Then I shall see Him face to face,
> To tell the story saved by grace.

Fanny Crosby wrote nearly 9,000 gospel poems, and her hymns will continue to be used as long as the gospel is sung.

The musical setting by George C. Stebbins enhances the beauty of the poem. It is another of his melodic gems which have endeared him to the hymn-loving public.

"I was blind, but now I see."

SOME DAY THE SILVER CORD WILL BREAK

(Saved by Grace)

Fanny J. Crosby

George C. Stebbins

1. Some day the sil - ver cord will break, And I no more as now shall sing;
2. Some day my earth - ly house will fall, I can - not tell how soon 'twill be,
3. Some day, when fades the golden sun Beneath the ros - y - tint - ed west,
4. Some day: till then I'll watch and wait, My lamp all trimmed and burning bright,

But Oh! the joy when I shall wake With - in the pal - ace of the King!
But this I know, my All - in - all Has now a place in heav'n for me.
My blessed Lord will say, "Well done!" And I shall en - ter in - to rest.
That when my Sav - iour opes the gate, My soul to Him may take its flight.

REFRAIN

And I shall see Him face to face, And tell the sto - ry, saved by grace;
shall see to face,

And I shall see Him face to face, And tell the story, saved by grace.
shall see to face,

LORD, I'M COMING HOME

"Other seed fell into good ground and brought forth, some an hundred fold," is the scriptural band of approval wound around this invitation song. Written to win the soul of one man for Christ, it has been used by the Holy Spirit to convict countless sinners and call them to repentance. The story of its writing follows:

William J. Kirkpatrick was leading the singing at the camp meeting at Rawlinsville, Pa. His assisting soloist possessed a voice of rare beauty. He expressed the pathos of emotional passages so persuasively as to move hearer to tears. This great gift Mr. Kirkpatrick coveted for Christ, for he knew his singing assistant was not a Christian.

One morning after the service Mr. Kirkpatrick, deeply concerned about the soul of this man, went to his tent and knelt in prayer. He prayed that God would give him a message that would convict this man of his sin, and show him his need of surrender to the Christ whom Kirkpatrick knew, loved, and served. He kept praying. After a while came the words,

> "Coming home, coming home,
> Never more to roam.
> Open wide thine arms of love,
> Lord, I'm coming home."

Then followed in rapid succession the verses, one after another. He finished the song, believing he had a message given by God. That evening Mr. Kirkpatrick handed his soloist the manuscript copy of the song, "Lord, I'm Coming Home." He sang it with his usual fervor and power of interpretation. This song became the instrument of the Holy Spirit to convict the singer of his sin and need of unconditional surrender to Christ. Thus, a song written to reach one man has brought thousands into the Kingdom.

> "I've wandered far away from God,
> Now I'm coming home.
> The paths of sin too long I've trod,
> Lord, I'm coming home."

"And the young man said, I will arise and go to my father."

LORD, I'M COMING HOME

W. J. K.

WM. J. KIRKPATRICK

1. I've wan-dered far a - way from God, Now I'm com-ing home;
2. I've wast - ed man - y pre - cious years, Now I'm com-ing home;
3. I've tired of sin and stray-ing, Lord, Now I'm com-ing home;
4. My soul is sick, my heart is sore, Now I'm com-ing home;

FINE

The paths of sin too long I've trod, Lord, I'm com-ing home.
I now re - pent with bit - ter tears, Lord, I'm com-ing home.
I'll trust Thy love, be - lieve Thy word, Lord, I'm com-ing home.
My strength re-new, my hope re-store, Lord, I'm com-ing home.

D. S.—O - pen wide Thine arms of love, Lord, I'm com-ing home.

CHORUS

D. S.

Com - ing home, com - ing home, Nev - er - more to roam,

SOMEBODY CARES

"Somebody Cares" is the direct result of preaching.

Good preaching has given us many of the church's best hymns, for spiritual soil when ploughed by good preaching receives gladly the seed of Biblical teaching which, warmed by apostolic fervor and watered with evangelistic zeal, brings forth a harvest of spiritual fruits. Not the least of this wide variety are the songs of worship; indeed, most of our negro spirituals are born during the preaching service. "The great need of this weary world is to know that somebody cares" was the sentence from her minister's sermon that burned itself into the mind of Fannie Edna Stafford.

It was in the year 1905, and her minister was preaching on the text "And His name shall be called Jesus, for He shall save His people from their sins." Late that Sunday night, the sermon still filling her mind, its fructifying process began as she turned over and over in her thought "the great need of this weary world is to know that somebody cares." She was deeply impressed that what she had heard was so true it needed wider hearing than that one sermon. She would increase its hearing through a poem. As a result, she wrote half of the hymn as it now appears. On the morrow she finished it, and sent it to The Christian Endeavor World, in Boston, which published it under her name.

This poem struck a responsive chord in the hearts of many who read it. As a result, it was reprinted in many publications, not all of which gave credit to her as the author. From one such publication Homer Rodeheaver, recognizing the merit of the poem as a Gospel song lyric, took the copy and gave it a musical setting that fits the words perfectly. It was a great joy to all concerned when Fannie Edna Stafford was found to be the author, and recognition made in all our publications.

Here we have a splendid gospel hymn, the result of preaching the Word. "God so loved the world . . ."

SOMEBODY CARES

FANNIE EDNA STAFFORD HOMER A. RODEHEAVER

1. Some-bod - y knows when your heart aches, And ev'rything seems to go wrong;
2. Some-bod - y cares when you're tempted, And your mind grows dizzy and dim;
3. Some-bod - y loves you when wea - ry; 'y Somebody loves you when strong;

Some-bod - y knows when the shadows Need chasing a - way with a song;
Some-bod - y cares when you're weakest, And farthest a - way from Him;
Al - ways is wait - ing to help you, He watches you—one of the throng

Some-bod - y knows when you're lonely, Tir - ed, dis-cour-aged and blue;
Some-bod - y grieves when you're fallen, You are not lost from His sight;
Need-ing His friendship so ho - ly, Need-ing His watch-care so true;

Some-bod-y wants you to know Him, And know that He dear - ly loves you.
Some-bod-y waits for your com - ing, And He'll drive the gloom from your night.
His name? We call His name Je - sus; He loves ev - 'ry- one, He loves you.

BEYOND THE SUNSET

"We were guests at Rainbow Point, Winona Lake, the home of Homer Rodeheaver, world famous song leader, with other members of the faculty of the Rodeheaver School of Music," writes Virgil Brock. "This guest house is famous for its superb location on the eastern side of Winona Lake. It offers, as you look westward across the water, the best view of the sunset. Mrs. Brock and I watched one of these never-to-be-forgotten scenes. To us it seemed matchless in its beauty. The rapidly changing shades, deepening hues and blending colors, impoverished our vocabulary in an attempt to describe it.

"From inadequate words we spoke of the artist's possibility of catching its beauty in the colors of his palette. We decided that he, too, would fall short. It would take the poet who sees beyond the sunset to penetrate to the truth behind what our eyes saw. There we stood entranced, enjoying the hospitality of the householder at Rainbow Point, and watched the Householder of heaven draw down the multicolored curtains over His latticed windows. Our rapture moved to the inescapable question, 'What lies beyond the wondrous sunset? What will it be like when our work is done and the experience of heaven begun?'

"So amid the afterglow of the sunset, and still in the wonderland of its beauty, the poem took form and was set to music. To us it seemed as if a light of truth streamed through that open western window into our hearts and became a song to answer our question."

"The heavens declare the glory of God; and the firmament showeth His handiwork."

BEYOND THE SUNSET

(Dedicated to Horace L. and Grace Pierce Burr)

VIRGIL P. BROCK

BLANCHE KERR BROCK

1. Be-yond the sun - set, O bliss-ful morn - ing, When with our
2. Be-yond the sun - set no clouds will gath - er, No storms will
3. Be-yond the sun - set a hand will guide me To God, the
4. Be-yond the sun - set, O glad re - un - ion, With our dear

Sav - iour heav'n is be - gun. Earth's toiling end - ed, O glorious
threat - en, no fears an - noy; O day of glad - ness, O day un-
Fa - ther, whom i a - dore; His glorious pres - ence, His words of
loved ones who've gone be - fore; In that fair homeland we'll know no

dawn - ing; Be-yond the sun - set, when day is done.
end - ing, Be-yond the sun - set, e - ter - nal joy!
wel - come, Will be my por - tion on that fair shore.
par - ting, Bey-ond the sun - set for ev - er - more!

LEAD ME TO CALVARY

Sacrificial service plants a garden in the heart. This labor of love flowers forth in endless beauty. "Lead Me to Calvary" is such a bloom.

The care of an invalid sister nearly all her adult life was the uncomplaining task of Jennie Hussey. During this time-devouring and strength-testing task, she wrote her many poems. They show keen understanding of the meaning of the Cross. She, too, carried a cross, so knew its joy and source of strength.

In "Lead Me to Calvary" she bares her love and loyalty to Christ. Through Gethsemane she has come to the rich possession of obedience and surrender. This made her service a joy, and not a burden.

The music by Wm. J. Kirkpatrick reveals a sympathetic insight into the meaning of the poem. Without a doubt this is one of the finest hymns of recent years.

The words born of sacrifice, the music one of the last before Christ called Mr. Kirkpatrick home, together make a hymn destined to live and bless the world with its message.

LEAD ME TO CALVARY

Jennie Evelyn Hussey   Wm. J. Kirkpatrick

1. King of my life, I crown Thee now, Thine shall the glo - ry be;
2. Show me the tomb where Thou wast laid, Ten - der-ly mourned and wept;
3. Let me like Ma - ry, thru the gloom, Come with a gift to Thee;
4. May I be will - ing, Lord, to bear Dai - ly my cross for Thee;

Lest I for-get Thy thorn-crowned brow, Lead me to Cal - va - ry.
An - gels in robes of light ar - rayed Guard-ed Thee whilst Thou slept.
Show to me now the emp - ty tomb, Lead me to Cal - va - ry.
E - ven Thy cup of grief to share, Thou hast borne all for me.

CHORUS

Lest I for-get Geth-sem - a - ne; Lest I for-get Thine ag - o - ny;

Lest I for-get Thy love for me, Lead me to Cal - va - ry.

I SHALL NOT BE MOVED

"I Shall Not Be Moved" is the spiritual fruit of the Family Altar. Following the reading of the First Psalm at morning devotions, Mr. Ackley's mother sent him to the corner store. The words, "I shall not be moved," suggested by the Bible Reading, kept ringing ceaselessly in his heart during his journey. He hurried home and talked with his father about writing a hymn based on the First Psalm. They examined carefully whether or not the theme "I shall not be moved" caught the teaching of the Psalm. They agreed it was feasible, and that it appropriately set forth a fundamental teaching of the Psalm. He set to work and finished the hymn, both words and music, in a short time. This hymn, first introduced by Charles Butler, a great gospel singer, has a remarkable history.

God has signally blessed this simple gospel song with its pertinent truth. Translated, it has been sung around the world in many tongues.

"I Shall Not Be Moved" has exerted a vast influence for Christ and His kingdom. It was the favorite gospel song of Dr. Reuben A. Torrey, founder of the Los Angeles Bible Institute, and world renowned preacher and scholar.

The reach and influence of the gospel message in song or story can not be measured.

"He shall be like a tree planted . . ."

I SHALL NOT BE MOVED

A. H. A.

Alfred H. Ackley

1. As a tree be - side the wa - ter Has the Sav - ior plant-ed me;
2. Tho' the tem - pest rage a-round me, Thro' the storm my Lord I see,
3. When by grief my heart is bro - ken, And the sunshine steals a - way,
4. When at last I stand be-fore Him, Oh what joy it will af - ford,

All my fruit shall be in sea - son, I shall live e - ter - nal - ly.
Point-ing up - ward to that ha - ven, Where my loved ones wait for me.
Then His grace, in mer - cy giv - en, Chang-es dark - ness in - to day.
Just to see the sin - ner ransomed, And be-hold my sov'reign Lord.

CHORUS

I shall not be moved,...... I shall not be moved;......
shall not be moved,   shall not be moved;

An-chored to the Rock of A - ges, I shall not be moved.

SOMEBODY KNOWS

" 'Somebody knows!' spoke the still, small voice in my heart that day on State street, Sharon, Pa.," said B. D. Ackley. "As I walked, thinking over some minor difficulties, with my thought moving from one trouble to another, like fingers on a rosary, my lips burst forth with the question which welled up within me, 'Well, who knows?' and instantly the answer flashed, 'Jesus knows all of your troubles, sorrows and woes!'

"Believing I had material for a song, I sought my brother, Alfred, who was visiting with me at the time. I told him of my experience, and gave him an outline for the poem. It was several days later when he brought me the completed lyric.

"The melody for the chorus came with the words 'Somebody Knows.' I took my brother into the Deforrest Piano Store and played the melody for him. Later, at the house, members of the Billy Sunday evangelistic party gathered 'round the piano. After many changes and helpful suggestions the finished product emerged."

SOMEBODY KNOWS

Alfred H. Ackley

B. D. Ackley

Legato

1. Fail - ing in strength when opprest by my foes, Somebody knows, Somebody knows;
2. Why should I fear when the care-bil-lows roll? Somebody knows, Somebody knows;
3. Wounded and helpless and sick with distress, Somebody knows, Somebody knows;

Wait - ing for some-one to ban-ish my woes, Some-bod-y knows,–'tis Je - sus.
When the deep shadows sweep o-ver my soul, Some-bod-y knows,–'tis Je - sus.
Long- ing for home and a mother's ca-ress, Some-bod-y knows,–'tis Je - sus.

Chorus or Quartet

Some-bod-y knows, Some-bod-y knows When I am tempted and tried by my foes;

He is the One who will keep me— Some-bod- y knows—'tis Je - sus.

THE NINETY AND NINE

"The Ninety and Nine" is a spiritual mosaic of Jesus Christ, the Good Shepherd. Elizabeth C. Clephane has woven the scripture into a poem of rare beauty. In forming this mosaic she took the scriptural descriptions of the Good Shepherd as the artisan takes the pieces of tile, putting each in its place and proper relationship, with the result a true and perfect product.

"The Ninety and Nine" reveals depth of insight, and a genius in selection of material. The mosaic shows architectural beauty of design and spiritual understanding of content.

Miss Clephane wrote the hymn for children. It was published in The Children's Hour in 1868. She passed to her reward the following year.

Ira D. Sankey set the poem to music in 1874, so the author of the lyrics missed the knowledge of how great an immediate blessing her poem was, and its later growth to world-wide popularity and use.

From a religious paper Mr. Sankey was reading, while traveling in Scotland, he had cut the poem and put it in his vest pocket. Following a powerful sermon in Edinburg, on the "Good Shepherd," Dwight L. Moody, the evangelist, asked Mr. Sankey to sing something suitable. Ira Sankey thought of the poem for which there had, as yet, been no music written. Drawing the poem from his pocket he placed it on the organ and struck the chord of A-flat. He followed on, composing as he went the very tune which remains unchanged to this day. The audience was greatly moved. Mr. Sankey, in telling of the occasion, says "Mr. Moody was in tears, and so was I."

"I am the Good Shepherd . . . come to seek and to save that which was lost."

The Ninety and Nine

Elizabeth C. Clephane

Ira D. Sankey

1. There were ninety and nine that safe - ly lay   In the shel-ter   of the
2. "Lord,   Thou hast here Thy nine-ty and nine; Are   they not enough for
3. But   none of the ransomed ev   -   er knew How deep were the waters
4. "Lord, whence are those blood-drops all the way That mark out the mountain's
5. But   all thro' the mountains, thun-der-riv'n, And up from the rock-y

fold,   But   one   was out on the hills a - way, Far   off from the
Thee?" But the Shep-herd made answer: "This of mine   Has wan-dered a-
crossed; Nor how dark was the night that the Lord passed thro' Ere He found His
track?" "They were shed for one who had gone a-stray Ere the Shepherd could
steep,   There a-rose a glad cry to the gate of heav'n, "Re - joice! I have

rit.

gates   of   gold— A - way on the moun - tains wild and bare, A-
way   from me, And al - tho'   the   road   be rough and steep, I
sheep that was lost.   Out in the des - ert He heard   its   cry—
bring   him back." "Lord, whence are Thy hands so rent and torn?" "They're
found   my sheep!" And the an - gels ech-oed a - round the throne, "Re-

way from the ten-der Shepherd's care, A-way from the ten - der Shep-herd's care.
go   to the des-ert to find my sheep, I   go to the des-ert to   find my sheep."
Sick   and helpless, and ready to die;   Sick and helpless, and ready to die.
pierced to - night by many a thorn; They're pierced to-night by man-y a thorn."
joice, for the Lord brings back His own! Re-joice, for the Lord brings back His own."

SOME DAY HE'LL MAKE IT PLAIN

"Hope springs eternal in the human breast" is the poetic general statement of a universal truth; but the Christian has a hope that transforms the dark hours into bright jewels of sustaining faith. "Some Day He'll Make It Plain" falls in this category.

A tragedy in the life of Adam Geibel, the blind composer, gave us this song. His daughter had married a young college graduate whose talents gave every promise of high success. He was in the steel company's open hearth department which handled the molten metal. He had expected to leave with his wife for the seashore on Good Friday to spend the Easter holiday, but the man who was to have taken over his work asked Dr. Geibel's son-in-law to continue through Friday and Saturday. This he readily consented to do. He sent his wife to the seashore with the promise to follow as soon as possible. That Good Friday, as the great conveyor full of molten metal moved across the room, something gave way. Tons of white hot metal spilled out of the vast pot and flew in all directions. Three men were killed outright. Dr. Geibel's son-in-law was fatally injured. It was a tragedy, indeed.

For days Dr. Geibel was disconsolate and heartbroken, but one day as he entered the office it was evident from his demeanor that the burden had lifted. He was happier than he had been. His words to us proved it. He said he had a message in his heart from the Heavenly Father, which said: "Some day you'll understand, some day it will be plain to you." On the strength of this revelation, he wrote the first stanza, the chorus, and composed the music. Then it was turned over to Lida Shivers Leech, widely known writer of gospel songs, who, after prayerful consideration, finished the poem. She conformed to Dr. Geibel's understanding, giving perfect unity to the lyric.

Here again the hope of the Christian shines through sorrow with a light confident and serene.

"Though He slay me, yet will I trust Him."

SOME DAY HE'LL MAKE IT PLAIN

Lida Shivers Leech

Adam Geibel

Solo, or all in unison

1. I do not know why oft 'round me My hopes all shattered seem to be;
2. I can-not tell the depth of love, Which moves the Father's heart a-bove;
3. Tho' tri-als come thro' passing days, My life will still be filled with praise;

God's perfect plan I can-not see, ... But some day I'll un-der-stand.
My faith to test, my love to prove, ... But some day I'll un-der-stand.
For God will lead thro' darkened ways , . But some day I'll un-der-stand.

CHORUS.

Some day He'll make it plain to me, Some day when I His face shall see;

Some day from tears I shall be free, For some day I shall un-der-stand.

HEARTACHES

"My son, my son!" moaned the heart-broken father of his stub-born, rebellious, defiant and impenitent boy — that boy who was so sin-hardened as to be impervious to all appeal. He had brought dis-grace upon his father's name. His punishment for crime meant in-carceration in the penitentiary. His profligacy and ultimate shame-ful tragedy not only caused his mother's untimely death but brought his father to where he stood in desperate need of more than hu-man aid.

"Kick him into the street," said a neighbor "I cannot," said his father, "he is my son." He loved him. He went to the Rev. A. H. Ackley, told his story, and together they prayed for the son's salva-tion. The father was comforted and strengthened, but the son re-mained impenitent and blatantly defiant. The numbing heartache and agony of the father for his profligate son were accentuated by a long term penitentiary sentence. The broken-hearted father turned to Jesus, the only source of help for heartache: "A very present help in time of trouble."

This vivid experience with a father's heartache was caught by Mr. Ackley in a poignant poem, and set to music.

HEARTACHES

A. H. A.

Rev. A. H. Ackley

1. When your heart is ach-ing, turn to Je - sus, He's the dear-est
2. There is joy for ev - 'ry blight-ing sor - row, Sweet re - lief for
3. Je - sus un - der-stands, what-e'er the trou - ble, And He waits to

Friend that you can know; You will find Him standing close beside you,
ev - 'ry bit - ter pain, Je - sus Christ is still the great Phy-si-cian,
heal your wound-ed soul; Will you trust His love so strong and tender,

Wait-ing peace and com-fort to be - stow. . .
No one ev - er sought His help in vain. . . . Heart-aches, take them all to
He a - lone can make your spir-it whole. . .

CHORUS

Je - sus, Go to Him to - day, do it now with-out de - lay; Heart-aches,

take them all to Je - sus, He will take your heartaches all a-way.
He will take them all a-way.

I BELONG TO THE KING

"I Belong to the King" was literally beaten out of a humble life by the flail of burdensome trials and afflictions.

Ida L. Reed, author of the hymn, rightly deserved to sing "I belong to the King." She was born and reared in the mountains of West Virginia. Her life was one long, continuous burden-bearing journey. For many years she was compelled to do the heavy and arduous work incident to farm life. This she did in support of an invalid and widowed mother.

Broken at last by the strenuous toil and privations, she was sorely afflicted and bed-ridden for years. Even then, in her hours of pain, she wrote poems for publishers to eke out a meager living. She was removed to a hospital in Washington, D. C., as a last resort, in the hope of prolonging her pain-wracked, yet beautiful, life. From her hospital bed of pain, she wrote the words of this poem.

"I Belong to the King" is a golden nugget from the mine of character of one of God's most humble children. For, as often the most beautiful flowers grow in inconspicuous places, so from the inner garden of one of the least of the children of the Lord there comes this flower of thought. This poem is deservedly popular and grows in favor with the passing years.

Maurice A. Clifton matched his high estimate of the poem by giving it an adequate musical setting. The song leaped into popularity and has earned a well-merited reputation. It has been a source of comfort, with a measure of satisfaction, that I was able to bring help to this deserving author. When the attention of the American Society of Composers, Authors and Publishers was called to a financial state that was short of life's bare necessities, they voted her a pension with a monthly allowance that banished anxiety, and assured comfort for the rest of her life.

"She hath done what she could."

I BELONG TO THE KING

Ida L. Reed

Maurice A. Clifton

Solo or Duet

1. I be-long to the King, I'm a child of His love, I shall dwell in His pal-ace so fair; For He tells of its bliss in yon heav-en a-bove, And His chil-dren its splen-dors shall share.

2. I be-long to the King, and He loves me I know, For His mer-cy and kind-ness, so free, Are un-ceas-ing-ly mine, wher-so-ev-er I go, And my ref-uge un-fail-ing is He.

3. I be-long to the King, and His prom-ise is sure, That we all shall be gath-ered at last In His king-dom a-bove, by life's wa-ters so pure, When this life with its tri-als is past.

Chorus

I be-long to the King, I'm a child of His love, And He nev-er for-sak-eth His own; He will call me some day to His pal-ace a-bove, I shall dwell by His glo-ri-fied throne.

WONDERFUL PEACE

Peace is frictionless motion, like the spiritual serenity which flows through this poem. This song is bathed in the beauty of a holy quietness. The movement is calm, stately, marking progress of the soul journeying homeward, content and unafraid. The whole song reflects the achievement of spiritual growth.

The origin and mission of the song shows how God uses things small and humble for great ends. It came into being on the occasion of a Methodist camp meeting near West Bend, Wis., August, 1889, conducted by W. G. Cooper, in his parish there.

The meeting was one described as "charged with spiritual power, felt by all who entered the camp grounds." Noise was hushed into quietness, and confusion was quelled into orderliness.

The evangelist, W. D. Cornell, was a born poet, as well as a preacher of exceptional ability. His diction was perfect, and his language poetic and beautiful. His spoken sentences flowed like a clear, sparkling brook.

One day while seated in the tent, Mr. Cornell, following a period of deep introspection, wrote down the thoughts with which his mind had been busied. They later proved to be parts of this hymn, "Wonderful Peace." Sinking again into introspective rumination, he arose, unwittingly dropped the written verses on the tent floor, and went out. When Mr. Cooper entered the tent an hour or two later he discovered the paper. He was fascinated by the theme and the accompanying verses. It so fitted his own thinking that he filled in and completed the poem. Then sitting down at the organ he composed the melody as it has since been sung.

This hymn then is the essence of an evangelistic camp meeting, so harmonious in work and endued with spiritual power that in the hearts of its leaders it flowered into "Wonderful Peace."

"By this shall all men know that ye are my disciples;
that ye love one another."

WONDERFUL PEACE

W. D. CORNELL. Alt.　　　　　　　　　　　　　　　　　W. G. COOPER

1. Far a-way in the depths of my spir-it to-night Rolls a
2. What a treas-ure I have in this won-der-ful peace, Bur-ied
3. I am rest-ing to-night in this won-der-ful peace, Rest-ing
4. And me-thinks when I rise to that Cit-y of peace, Where the
5. Ah! soul, are you here with-out com-fort or rest, March-ing

mel - o - dy sweet-er than psalm; In ce - les - tial-like strains it un-
deep in the heart of my soul; So se - cure that no pow - er can
sweet-ly in Je - sus' con - trol; For I'm kept from all dan - ger by
Au - thor of peace I shall see, That one strain of the song which the
down the rough pathway of time? Make Je - sus your friend ere the

ceas - ing - ly falls O'er my soul like an in - fi - nite calm.
mine it a - way, While the years of e - ter - ni - ty roll.
night and by day, And His glo - ry is flood-ing my soul.
ran-somed will sing, In that heav - en - ly king-dom shall be:
shad-ows grow dark; Oh, ac - cept this sweet peace so sub - lime.

CHORUS

Peace! peace! won-der-ful peace, Com-ing down from the Fa-ther a - bove; Sweep

o - ver my spir-it for - ev - er, I pray, In fath-om-less bil-lows of love.

I MUST TELL JESUS

"I must tell Jesus" is the first confession of a penitent, and then a passionate cry for help. Rev. Elisha A. Hoffman was summoned to help a friend who was in great trouble. He tried to comfort her by telling of the unfailing love of God. He spoke of that love which brought us into being, and follows us every step of our way. He urged her to surrender to God's mercy, and told her the help she needed could only come when she was fully repentant. He prayed earnestly for her, and while he was praying she suddenly screamed, "I must tell Jesus!" His pastoral visit, spiritual instruction and earnest prayer led to her conversion, and she became a great soul winner in the Master's service.

"I must tell Jesus" was wrought out of a minister's intimate dealing with a soul seeking succor from sickness and sin. His tender ministry of quoted scripture promises, "Come unto me all ye that labor and are heavy laden and I will give you rest; if ye confess your sins He is faithful and just to forgive; cast thy burden on the Lord, and He will sustain thee," and his earnest prayer for God's blessing on her body and soul brought forth the great confession, "I must tell Jesus!" She needed healing for her body, peace for her mind, and assurance in her soul, so she cried out from the very depths of her being. Such a cry God always answers.

Deeply impressed by this experience, Mr. Hoffman wrote the poem and music. It contrasts with other gospel songs in that it is entirely a great confession—the kind of confession that leads into and flows out of salvation.

"If thou shalt confess with thy mouth the Lord Jesus,
and shalt believe in thine heart . . . thou shalt be saved."

I MUST TELL JESUS

Elisha A. Hoffman

Elisha A. Hoffman

1. I must tell Jesus all of my trials; I cannot bear these
2. I must tell Jesus all of my troubles; He is a kind, com-
3. Tempted and tried I need a great Saviour, One who can help my
4. O how the world to evil allures me! O how my heart is

burdens alone; In my distress He kindly will help me;
passionate Friend; If I but ask Him, He will deliver,
burdens to bear; I must tell Jesus, I must tell Jesus;
tempted to sin! I must tell Jesus, and He will help me

CHORUS

He ever loves and cares for His own.
Make of my troubles quickly an end. I must tell Jesus!
He all my cares and sorrows will share.
Over the world the victory to win.

I must tell Jesus! I cannot bear my burdens alone; I must tell

Jesus! I must tell Jesus! Jesus can help me, Jesus alone.

INTO MY HEART

"My sins are mightier than I" is the tragic knowledge of the confirmed drunkard. There is no defeat so bitter as the discovery to a man that he has sold his soul unto sin. He faces this fact within himself — abysmal, hopeless despair, for his sin defeats his best efforts to unshackle his chain of habit. All that can be done for him that is humanly possible falls before the devastating power of this destroying habit. Only a new heart can bring release, with new life and new hope. So we understand why the drunkard at the altar, seeking a way out of his sin, cried out, "Come into my heart, Lord Jesus, come in to stay!"

During an evangelistic campaign in the Trinity Evangelical Church at Shamokin, Pa., a man obviously under the influence of liquor responded to the altar call. He had been deeply moved by the strong evangelistic message. He felt his need of a Saviour. Tired of his bondage to sin, he sought a way out. Good friends of the church prayed for him; they told him of Jesus the Mighty to save, Who came to save sinners, and Who was able to save to the uttermost all who come unto Him. Immediately the penitent cried out, "Come into my heart, Lord Jesus, come in to stay!" Out of that experience, Harry D. Clarke, the evangelist, wrote this winsome prayer chorus. It is a song of liberation.

"Whosoever the Son shall set free, shall be free indeed."

INTO MY HEART

Harry D. Clarke   Harry D. Clarke

1. Come in-to my heart, bless-ed Je-sus, Come in-to my heart, I pray;
2. Come in-to my heart, bless-ed Je-sus, I need Thee thro' life's drear-y way;
3. Come in-to my heart, bless-ed Je-sus, And take all my guilt a-way;
4. Come in-to my heart, bless-ed Je-sus, O cleanse and il-lu-mine my soul;

My soul is so troub-led and wea-ry, Come in-to my heart to-day.
The bur-den of sin is so heav-y, Come in-to my heart to stay.
Then spotless I'll stand in Thy pres-ence, When breaks Thine e-ter-nal day.
Fill me with Thy won-der-ful Spir-it, Come in and take full con-trol.

Chorus

In-to my heart, in-to my heart, Come in-to my heart, Lord Je - sus;

Come in to-day, Come in to stay, Come in-to my heart, Lord Je - sus.

MOTHER'S PRAYERS HAVE FOLLOWED ME

Mrs. Lizzie DeArmond put a mother's deep concern for a son's welfare into this lyric. She penned the poem for a boy in her Sunday School class of the Presbyterian Church in Swarthmore, Pa. This boy, filled with the spirit of wanderlust and adventure, had determined to leave his home to see the world. He was too young and unprepared to do this. He needed his home and mother's influence for a number of years more. Mrs. DeArmond knowing this, sought to dissuade him from such a step. She was not only a friend of the family, but the boy's Sunday School teacher. She used every argument that would appeal to a boy's heart and mind, but to no avail. He left his home. So she wrote this song to reach a boy and bring him back home again to his mother, and, far more important, to God. I cannot attest to the song's success in this individual case, but God has used this simple message as the means of saving many boys who had left home and God.

Mrs. DeArmond assumes correctly in her poem that mothers have more to do in determining the destiny of their children than any other human agency. This song has no thought of the weak sentimentality and indulgence often mistaken for love, but rather fearless Christian discipline, sturdy, strong, rigid as steel, woven with the enduring fibers of eternity. This understanding has made Mrs. DeArmond's poem an effectual message for righteousness.

B. D. Ackley sensed the spirit of the poem and composed a pleading type of melody which has heightened the song's success.

> "Woman, behold thy son! . . . Son,
> behold thy mother!"

MOTHER'S PRAYERS HAVE FOLLOWED ME

Lizzie DeArmond.

B. D. Ackley

1. I grieved my Lord from day to day, I scorned His love so full and free, And though I wan-dered far a-way, My moth-er's pray'rs have fol-lowed me.
2. O'er des-ert wild, o'er mountain high A wan-der-er I chose to be, A wretch-ed soul con-demned to die, Still moth-er's pray'rs have fol-lowed me.
3. He turned my dark-ness in-to light, This bless-ed Christ of Cal-va-ry, I'll praise His name both day and night, That moth-er's pray'rs have fol-lowed me.

REFRAIN.

I'm com-ing home, I'm com-ing home, To live my wast-ed life a-new, For moth-er's pray'rs have fol-lowed me, Have fol-lowed me the whole world thro'.

AT THE END OF THE ROAD

A disappointed fisherman caught few fish on his hook one day, but his heart won and captured a song. This favorite song of the author, Rev. Alfred Henry Ackley, resulted from one of those fishing trips, aptly described as "fisherman's luck." Mr. Ackley, like his father before him, was a fisherman. As a fisherman he felt he belonged to a great and glorious company. Yet being a fisherman does not guarantee a full creel, a fact he overlooked one day in the Pocono Mountains of Pennsylvania. From sun-up to sun-down he fished, but caught nothing. His favorite fishing hole had been "cleaned out." In the gathering twilight three small trout were his total catch.

That homeward walk through the gathering dusk over the corduroy road, speckled with shadows of the coming night, his creel with three small fish was heavy as lead, for light is the full creel, and leaden an empty one. Disappointed, tired and hungry, he trudged the lonely road, thinking of the welcome that awaited him at home. His thought lifts as he mused on the everlasting joys that God has for His children as they reach the end of life's road. Worn out, he reached home, too tired to do anything but eat and sleep.

The next day he took up a study of the theme and wrote "At the End of the Road." He caught few fish, but he became ensnared in a song. He had that greatest of life's joys — joining with God in making a Symphony of Life out of the day's discords and disappointments.

"Follow me, and I will make you fishers of men."

AT THE END OF THE ROAD

A. H. A.

Rev. A. H. Ackley

1. There'll be light in the sky, from the pal-ace on high, When I come to the end of the road; . . . Sweet re-lief from all care will be wait-ing me there,
2. Ev - 'ry long wea-ry mile I'll re-count with a smile, When I come to the end of the road, . . . And the foes that be - set, God will make me for-get,
3. Just a gate o - pen wide and a friend by my side, When I come to the end of the road, . . . That is all that I ask as a crown for my task,

When I come to the end of the road. . . .

REFRAIN

When the long day is end-ed, the jour-ney is o'er, I shall en-ter that bless-ed a-bode, . . . For the Sav-ior I love will be wait-ing for me When I come to the end of the road.

JESUS, I AM COMING HOME

"Religion makes the common things beautiful. The everyday, oft-repeated commonplace experience takes on significance and holds a new and different meaning when we are right with God," said B. D. Ackley. He was telling me the attention-arresting story of how "Jesus, I Am Coming Home" came to be written.

"The clicking of the wheels on the rail joints of a stuffy day coach in which I was riding became so audible, and had such a persistently intrusive note, I found myself keeping time with the rhythmic clicks. I shifted from one thought to another, seeking to find a suitable phrase to match the rail-rhythm. All this without any definite ideas for a melody. Of course, the fact that I was hurrying home between meetings at Danville, Ill., and Bellingham, Wash., focused my attention on my home, for I would not get to see my youngest daughter, then three months old, unless I left the Danville campaign Thursday before its close. This I did, and though the train out of Terre Haute carried no parlor car, that old stuffy day coach clicked out a matching rhythm to the idea fixed in my mind, 'Well, I'm coming home today.' On the little pad which I invariably carried with me in those days, I jotted down the idea and the melody which accompanied it, suggested with words beaten out by the car-clicking wheels on the rails.

"My brother, A. H. Ackley, to whom I immediately sent the manuscript, wrote the words on the theme, and to the melody I sent him. I took the song with me when we opened the Billy Sunday meetings at New Castle, Pa., in 1910."

This song has proved to be a very effective invitation song for evangelistic services.

"Surely goodness and mercy shall follow me . . . and I shall dwell in the house of the Lord forever."

JESUS, I AM COMING HOME

A. H. ACKLEY

B. D. ACKLEY

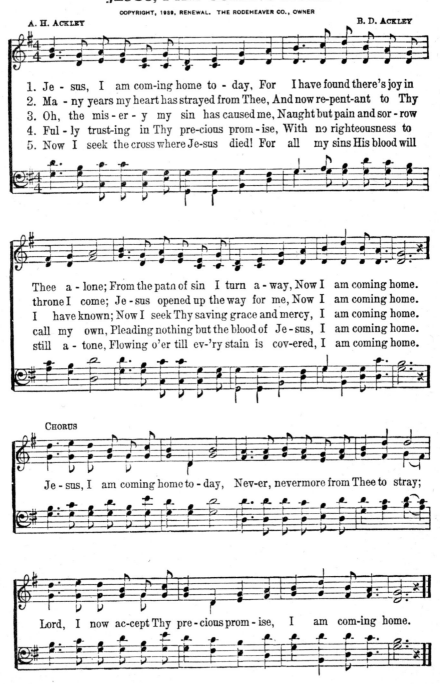

1. Je - sus, I am com-ing home to - day, For   I have found there's joy in
2. Ma - ny years my heart has strayed from Thee, And now re-pent-ant to Thy
3. Oh, the mis - er - y my sin has caused me, Naught but pain and sor - row
4. Ful - ly trust-ing in Thy pre-cious prom - ise, With no righteousness to
5. Now I seek the cross where Je-sus died! For   all   my sins His blood will

Thee a - lone; From the path of sin I turn a - way, Now I am coming home.
throne I come; Je - sus opened up the way for me, Now I am coming home.
I have known; Now I seek Thy saving grace and mercy, I am coming home.
call my own, Pleading nothing but the blood of Je - sus, I am coming home.
still a - tone, Flowing o'er till ev-'ry stain is cov-ered, I am coming home.

CHORUS

Je - sus, I am coming home to - day, Nev-er, nevermore from Thee to stray;

Lord, I now ac-cept Thy pre - cious prom - ise, I   am com-ing home.

THE CHURCH BY THE SIDE OF THE ROAD

This song is the recognition of a deep debt, a debt of gratitude for the wholesomeness of village life. Rev. William C. Poole had watched the lives of many who had left the country for the great city. They seemed to stand firm against the many temptations they met. The contributions to their lives by the home, church and school of the country were invaluable assets; as life tested them they gave evidence of being deeply rooted in the fundamental virtues of a good life. His own tender memories of boyhood training in a small town are also in this poem.

On the eastern shore of Maryland, W. C. Poole pointed out to me the little white church at the crossroads which had made his heart rich — rich in faith in God, and in love for his fellowman. Near by was the "little red school-house" where the mind was furnished with the knowledge for a career. A little beyond was the well kept cemetery, where reposed the bodies of the countryside's beloved dead. So he had visual evidence of the emphasis placed on the various phases of country life: The church for the care of the soul; the school for the culture of the mind; the resting-place for the bodies of loved ones, showing reverence for those of the home. "It was a good program for a successful life," he said; "respect for the body, training of mind, and schooling of the spirit.

So the memories of his own worthy rootage of prayer at mother's knee, of church, and of school, combined with rural environment, are responsible for this poem. Good soil, good seed, and a good harvest.

B. D. Ackley matched the spirit of the poem in the melody.

THE CHURCH BY THE SIDE OF THE ROAD

Rev. W. C. Poole

B. D. Ackley

1. Thro' the mist of years I can seem to see The church of my childhood
2. And the old, old songs that we used to sing, I'm sing-ing them o'er and
3. At   the place of pray'r, in that lit - tle church, I knelt at my mother's
4. There's a hal-lowed spot 'neath the old pine tree, Where mother was laid to

days; And it's mem-'ries sweet, so with joy re - plete, Shall live in my
o'er; They give strength and cheer, when the clouds draw near, And lead to the
side, There the Lord I found, it is ho - ly ground, The One who for
rest; What a joy 'twill be   her dear face to   see, With Him that I

CHORUS. (*First four measures old melody.*)

heart al - way.
oth - er shore. Then on mem - o - ry's page I can see   a - gain, The
sin - ners died.
love the best.

church by the side of the road;   And wher-ev - er   I

roam, it   is guid-ing me home, The church by the side of the road.

IS IT THE CROWNING DAY?

"The good that men do lives after them" is true of the writer of this song. Rev. Henry Ostrom will continue to bring to many audiences a real inspiration in his song, "Glad Day," even after he has left us for a while. He has heard the call, "Well done, good and faithful servant, enter thou into the joy of thy Lord." He has blessed us with a song, but he also bequeathed us a becoming modesty.

I secured this song at Winona Lake, Ind., in 1910, but it was not until twenty-five years later, at Collingswood, N. J., that any audience knew who was the author. The poem credited to George Walker Whitcomb was the work of Dr. Ostrom. He modestly hid behind the pseudonym of "Whitcomb." He used the hymn in all his evangelistic campaigns. He felt a greater freedom in its use under another's name as author.

In 1935, while he was holding a Bible conference in my own home church, at Collingswood, N. J., I asked the audience if they would like to see the author of the hymn, "Is It the Crowning Day?" which we had just sung. It was then I had the pleasure of revealing the real author of this great hymn.

When the hymn was first introduced at the conference session of the Seibert United Evangelical Church, Allentown, Pa., it was received with great enthusiasm. This instant popularity rose by leaps and bounds, until it has become the widest used song on **The Second Coming.**

"I will come again and receive you unto myself."

Is It the Crowning Day?

George Walker Whitcomb

Charles H. Marsh

1. Je - sus may come to - day, Glad day! Glad day! And I would
2. I may go home to - day, Glad day! Glad day! Seem - eth I
3. Why should I anx - ious be? Glad day! Glad day! Lights ap - pear
4. Faithful I'll be to - day, Glad day! Glad day! And I will

see my Friend; Dan - gers and trou - bles would end If
hear their song; Hail to the ra - di - ant throng! If
on the shore, Storms will af - fright nev - er - more, For
free - ly tell Why I should love Him so well, For

Chorus

Je - sus should come to - day.
I should go home to - day.
He is "at hand" to - day. Glad day! Glad day! Is it the crowning
He is my all to - day.

day? I'll live for to - day, nor anx - ious be, Je - sus, my Lord, I

rit.

soon shall see; Glad day! Glad day! Is it the crown-ing day?

DOES JESUS CARE

The touch of God's sympathetic understanding and help gave us this intimate confession of Rev. Frank E. Graeff. His heart-warming experience of the Divine Presence as he went through deep waters was like the Psalmist's "From the deep and miry pit He lifted me." He had suffered the feeling of being abandoned as trial after trial tested his faith, and burden upon burden was laid upon his shoulders. In this extremity he turned his thoughts to Jesus Christ; and, whereas it had seemed as if he could bear no more, he now became conscious of a presence filling him with strength. He felt his burdens grow lighter, other shoulders took some of the load. This sense of sympathy and of burden-sharing flooded his heart with joyous strength. It arrested that loss of spiritual power which seeps from the bleeding heart.

This personal touch became salve to his wounds. Soon his confidence was restored and new strength begotten. He won again his lost joy, and his life advanced to higher goals with wider horizon. This touch of God's helping hand in sympathetic understanding made him a richer personality, gave him a keener understanding, and made a more helpful, sympathetic pastor and friend to all people. He could scarcely help writing in trumpeting triumph, "I know He cares! I know my Saviour cares!"

While Mr. Graeff served some of the leading churches of the Philadelphia Methodist Conference, he was known as the "Sunshine Minister."

All those who suffer much can find deeper joy. Deep-throated, joyous laughter wells up from the heart which has discovered not only blessed relief but adequate help for hitherto unbearable burdens. The ineffable joy of Jesus' touch pervades this song: "O yes, He cares, I know He cares!"

Mr. J. Lincoln Hall gave prayerful consideration to the theme of the poem and wrote the melody in beautiful, touching strains.

DOES JESUS CARE

Frank E. Graeff

J. Lincoln Hall

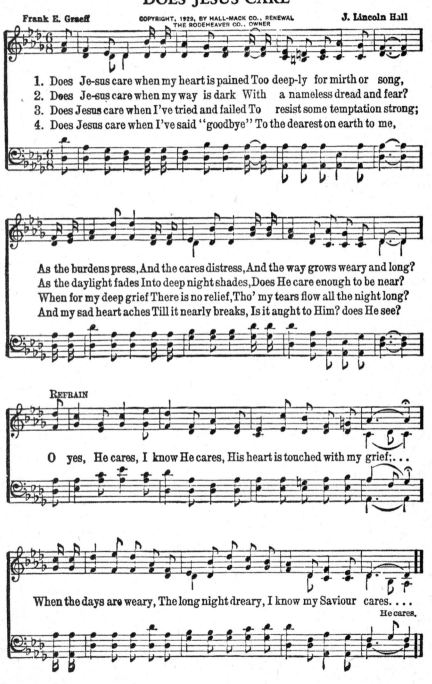

1. Does Je-sus care when my heart is pained Too deep-ly for mirth or song,
2. Does Je-sus care when my way is dark With a nameless dread and fear?
3. Does Jesus care when I've tried and failed To resist some temptation strong;
4. Does Jesus care when I've said "goodbye" To the dearest on earth to me,

As the burdens press, And the cares distress, And the way grows weary and long?
As the daylight fades Into deep night shades, Does He care enough to be near?
When for my deep grief There is no relief, Tho' my tears flow all the night long?
And my sad heart aches Till it nearly breaks, Is it aught to Him? does He see?

REFRAIN

O yes, He cares, I know He cares, His heart is touched with my grief;...

When the days are weary, The long night dreary, I know my Saviour cares. ...

He cares.

I NEED JESUS

Quiet contemplation, followed by self-examination, gave us the song, "I Need Jesus."

Rev. George O. Webster, who wrote the poem, was a guest in the home of Dr. E. S. Lorenz, on Brant Lake in the Adirondacks, where I asked him how he received his theme for his song, "I Need Jesus." He said that while sitting on the porch of his own cottage one afternoon he thought over the various aspects of the Kingdom of God. He thought it foolish for Christians to be unhappily divided. He recognized the legitimacy of different branches of the church, but antagonistic divisions within he deplored.

"After all," ran his thought, "we all need Jesus, the ultra-liberal as well as the ultra-conservative needs Jesus. As I look into my own heart, 'I need Jesus'." It was when he looked into his own heart, and saw his first and fundamental need was Jesus, like that of everyone in the world, that the song was born.

Like all great confessions, this song indicates the richness of the spiritual experience behind it. For confessions like "I Need Jesus" reveal great depths; it recalls Peter's "Thou art the Christ, the Son of the living God." So true confessions are signs of the depth of recognition and completeness of surrender. Confession of Christ means surrender to Him, even as confession of sin clearly means having surrendered to wrong. This song then is a glad and triumphant surrender to Jesus Christ; it was so conceived. May it be sung likewise!

Charles H. Gabriel has enriched this poem with a musical setting of rare beauty.

I NEED JESUS

George O. Webster

Chas. H. Gabriel

1. I need Je-sus, my need I now con-fess; No friend like Him in times of deep dis-tress; I need Je-sus, the need I glad-ly own; Tho' some may bear their load a-lone, Yet I need Je-sus.

2. I need Je-sus, I need a friend like Him, A friend to guide when paths of life are dim; I need Je-sus when foes my soul as-sail; A-lone I know I can but fail,– So I need Je-sus.

3. I need Je-sus, I need Him to the end; No one like Him—He is the sin-ners' Friend; I need Je-sus, no oth-er friend will do; So con-stant, kind, so strong, and true,–Yes, I need Je-sus.

CHORUS

I need Je-sus, I need Je-sus, I need Je-sus with me, I need Je-sus al-ways, I need Je-sus ev-'ry day; . . . . ev-'ry day; Need Him in the sun-shine hour, Need Him when the storm-clouds low'r; Ev-'ry day a-long my way, Yes, I need Je-sus.

SING AND SMILE AND PRAY

Rain may keep the crowd away, yet be the means of a greater hearing than if the crowd had come, thus a present loss becomes a future gain.

On the day of a special Young People's meeting, during evangelistic services by Virgil P. and Blanche Kerr Brock, a violent rainstorm lasted all day and far into the night. Their carefully laid plans for an overflow meeting of young people to hear a vital message were frustrated; it seemed that the opportunity to largely service the young people was lost.

As the day wore on, and the rain did not cease, the Brocks began to wonder what they would do should the rain continue and keep the expected crowd away. Meditation on this thought resulted in writing the chorus of this song. Regardless of the number in attendance, they would *sing* and praise God. Even if the weather cut down the attendance, they could *smile* and thank God for the many other well-attended meetings. Best of all, they would *pray* and redeem the time.

So in this prosaic way was composed the chorus which has rung across our land: "Sing and Smile and Pray." It was well-named by that Christian Professor of Chemistry, "A Spiritual Catalyst for Optimism" — mix it with any difficult situation, and you produce a smiling result.

"A merry heart doeth good like a medicine."

SING AND SMILE AND PRAY

Dedicated to our good friend, Homer A. Rodeheaver

Virgil P. Brock

Blanche Kerr Brock

1. Sing the clouds a - way, night will turn to day; If you sing and
2. Smile the clouds a - way, night will turn to day; If you smile and
4. Sing and smile and pray, that's the on - ly way; If you sing and

sing and sing, You'll sing the clouds a - way.
smile and smile, You'll smile the clouds a - way.   3. Pray the clouds a - way,
smile and pray, You'll drive the clouds a - way.

FINE.

D. C. 4th Verse

Pray and pray and pray; Night will turn to day, No mat-ter what they say.

WHERE THE GATES SWING OUTWARD NEVER

"Dad," said Charles H. Gabriel, Jr., from the embrace of his father, "if I never see you again here, I'll meet you where the gates never swing outward." His father, the beloved song writer, had gone to New York to bid his son God-speed as he departed for France during the First World War. It was while clasped in that last good-bye, his eyes turned toward the gates through which he must pass to go on shipboard. Those gates of entrance to war and death swung both ways; it gave him an apt figure of speech to phrase his parting from his father.

"I'll meet you where the gates never swing outward!" The words sketched a picture in the mind of his father, who, while the train journeyed westward toward his Chicago home, held in his heart his son's heart-warming good-bye message of love and filial affection. From his meditation came this tender song: "Where the gates swing outward never!"

WHERE THE GATES SWING OUTWARD NEVER

C. H. G.

CHAS. H. GABRIEL

1. Just a few more days to be filled with praise, And to tell the
2. Just a few more years with their toil and tears, And the jour - ney
3. Tho' the hills be steep and the val - leys deep, With no flow'rs my
4. What a joy 'twill be when I wake to see Him for whom my

old, old sto - ry; Then, when twi - light falls, and my Sav - ior calls.
will be end - ed; Then I'll be with Him, where the tide of time
way a - dorn - ing; Tho' the night be lone and my rest a stone.
heart is burn - ing! Nev - er-more to sigh, nev - er-more to die—

CHORUS

I shall go to Him in glo - ry.
With e - ter - ni - ty is blend - ed. I'll exchange my cross for a
Joy a - waits me in the morn - ing.
For that day my heart is yearn - ing.

star - ry crown, Where the gates swing outward nev - er; At His feet I'll

lay ev - 'ry bur - den down, And with Je - sus reign for - ev - er.

IF YOUR HEART KEEPS RIGHT

"I prefer songs that have a bright, cheery message, that will lift people out of clouds of doubt, songs that give messages of hope and comfort." This was Mr. Ackley's reply to Mrs. Lizzie DeArmond's question as to the style of songs he preferred. "If Your Heart Keeps Right" resulted from this conversation.

Mrs. DeArmond, who lived in Swarthmore, Pa., knew from experience the truth penned by the poet, "Into each life some rain must fall," for she had many clouds in her own life, had weathered many storms, and endured testing trials and tribulations. She had triumphed over her difficulties, for she knew that every cloud would wear a rainbow if your heart keeps right. From the laboratory of her own experience she brought forth this excellent spiritual formula for curing troubled lives: If your heart keeps right.

This song was introduced at Scranton, Pa., in 1913, during the Billy Sunday evangelistic campaign. Mrs. DeArmond had the pleasure of hearing her song joyously sung by the vast audiences of the evangelistic campaign. It is preeminently what it purports to be—a song to bring hope and cheer. As such, it has lifted the spirits of millions 'round the world.

The wings of melodious music given the poem by B. D. Ackley have heightened its success to an unusual degree. A poem always has the power of its own inherent beauty of conception; add the universal appeal of appropriate musical setting and you multiply that power. Mr. Ackley has done just that for Mrs. DeArmond's poem.

"Give me thine heart."

IF YOUR HEART KEEPS RIGHT

Lizzie DeArmond

B. D. Ackley

1. If the dark shad-ows gath-er As you go a - long, Do not grieve for their
2. Is your life just a tan - gle Full of toil and care? Smile a bit as you
3. There are blos-soms of glad-ness 'Neath the win- ter's snow, From the gloom and the

com-ing, Sing a cheer-y song; There is joy for the tak-ing, It will soon be light—
jour-ney, Oth- ers' bur-dens share; You'll for-get all your troubles, Mak-ing their lives bright,
darkness Comes the morning's glow; Nev- er give up the bat -tle, You will win the fight,

CHORUS

Ev - 'ry cloud wears a rain-bow If your heart keeps right. If your heart keeps right, If your
Skies will grow blue and sun- ny If your heart keeps right.
Gain the rest of the Vic- tor, If your heart keeps right.

heart keeps right, There's a song of glad-ness in the dark-est night; If your heart keeps right,

If your heart keeps right, Ev -'ry cloud will wear a rain-bow, If your heart keeps right.

WHEN THE ROLL IS CALLED UP YONDER

The elements of a true gospel song are always of life's common experiences plus the touch of God. Here we have a Sunday School teacher using an alley for a short cut to the post office, passing a drunkard's home of dire poverty. He asked a young, ill-clad girl, sweeping a porch, to come to Sunday School. The clothing, she tearfully said she lacked, was furnished by his wife and two Christian friends. Then followed Sunday School and Epworth League, steady attendance, and a memorable Roll Call meeting. At this meeting repeated calling of the girl's name to respond to the roll call of attendance met stony silence. Of such materials the theme and song, "When the Roll is Called Up Yonder," were made.

James M. Black, teacher of the Sunday School class in a Methodist church, Williamsport, Pa., and leader of the Epworth League, was a song leader of exceptional ability, and closed each League meeting with an appropriate song, planned to impress some outstanding truth upon the hearts of the young people. When Bessie failed to respond to several roll calls, he searched the song book for a suitable message. He found none and closed the impressive Roll Call meeting, feeling an opportunity had gone forever.

In telling of the incident, Mr. Black said: "This lack of a fitting song caused me both sorrow and disappointment. An inner voice seemed to say, 'Why don't you write one?' I put away the thought. As I opened the gate on my way home, the same thought came again so strongly that tears filled my eyes. I entered the house and sat down at the piano. The words came to me effortlessly: 'When the trumpet of the Lord shall sound, and time shall be no more; and the morning breaks eternal, bright and fair; when the saved of earth shall gather over on the other shore, and the roll is called up yonder, I'll be there.' The tune came the same way — I dared not change a note or word." The subsequent death of the girl from pneumonia, after an illness of ten days, furnished the dramatic finale which gives a poignancy to this Roll Call song.

WHEN THE ROLL IS CALLED UP YONDER

J. M. B.   J. M. Black

1. When the trump-et of the Lord shall sound, and time shall be no more, And the
2. On that bright and cloudless morn-ing when the dead in Christ shall rise, And the
3. Let us la - bor for the Mas - ter from the dawn till set - ting sun, Let us

morning breaks, e- ter - nal, bright and fair; When the saved of earth shall gath-er o - ver
glo - ry of His res - ur- rec- tion share; When His cho - sen ones shall gath-er to their
talk of all His wondrous love and care; Then when all of life is o - ver, and our

CHORUS

on the oth - er shore, And the roll is called up yon - der, I'll be there.
home be-yond the skies, And the roll is called up yon - der, I'll be there. When the
work on earth is done, And the roll is called up yon - der, I'll be there.

roll .... is called up yon - der, When the roll .... is called up yon - der,
When the roll is called up yon-der, I'll be there,   When the roll is called up yon-der, I'll be there,

When the roll .... is called up yon- der, When the roll is called up yon-der, I'll be there.
When the roll is called up yon - der,

I'LL GO WHERE YOU WANT ME TO GO

"Can you sing me a verse of my favorite song, without the music?" queried John D. Rockefeller, Sr., of Homer Rodeheaver, as Mr. Rockefeller was ready to tee off at his Ormond, Fla., golf course. "Yes," said Mr. Rodeheaver, and that song was "I'll Go Where You Want Me to Go." This is not strange, for not only in the life of the multi-millionaire, but in numberless other lives have the gospel songs had a profound and far-reaching effect.

Not enough has been written of the contribution made to Christian character by the music of the church; and far too little has been brought forward of the amazingly large influence of the gospel songs. Let me present a pencil sketch outline of three lives influenced by this one song — three lives, three leaders, three outstanding personalities definitely changed and vitally influenced by one song. Their lives have made large contributions to their day and generation. The tremendous impact upon their day for God and righteousness is a small sample of the work of the gospel song.

The first urge to become a gospel singer came to Homer Rodeheaver at the hearing of Mary Brown's song, "I'll Go Where You Want Me to Go." He left the mountains of East Tennessee to attend Ohio Wesleyan at Delaware, Ohio, in 1897, where he heard a singer named Ellis sing this song. Since that time he has reached the top rung of gospel song, and has sung the gospel message all over the world. Grace Moore, famous star of cinema, the network, and grand opera, told a nation-wide audience of the deep and abiding influence this song had in her life. Not only was it her first solo in her little mountain church in Jellico, Tenn., but is also her favorite hymn. Charles M. Alexander, another son of the Tennessee mountains, was influenced profoundly by this song. Much of the vast influence he wielded as a song leader looks backward to the early effects of Mary Brown's song.

Mrs. Carrie E. Rounsefell, Boston, Mass., wrote the music. In her evangelistic work she played the zither to accompany her singing. The words of the song, handed to her by a friend, suggested the tune she struck on her zither. This was later published and sent on its helpful mission to bless the world.

"By their fruits ye shall know them."

I'LL GO WHERE YOU WANT ME TO GO

Mary Brown

Carrie E. Rounsefell

1. It may not be on the mountain height, Or o-ver the storm-y sea, It may not
2. Per-haps to-day there are lov-ing words Which Je-sus would have me speak; There may be
3. There's surely somewhere a low-ly place In earth's harvest fields so wide, Where I may

be at the bat-tle's front My Lord will have need of me; But if, by a still, small
now in the paths of sin Some wand'rer whom I should seek: O Sav-iour, if Thou wilt
la-bor thru life's short day For Je-sus, the Cru-ci-fied; So trust-ing my all to Thy

voice He calls To paths that I do not know, I'll answer, dear Lord, with my hand in Thine, I'll
be my guide, Tho' dark and rug-ged the way, My voice shall ech-o the message sweet, I'll
ten-der care, And knowing Thou lov-est me, I'll do Thy will with a heart sin-cere, I'll

REFRAIN

go where you want me to go.
say what you want me to say. I'll go where you want me to go, dear Lord, Over mountain, or
be what you want me to be.

plain, or sea; I'll say what you want me to say, dear Lord, I'll be what you want me to be.

SAVED TO THE UTTERMOST

Captured in the crisp phrase, "Saved to the uttermost," is the picture of William J. Kirkpatrick. An insight into the character of the author of so many great spiritual messages is in this song which he wrote for the young people of old Ebenezer Methodist Church, Philadelphia, Pa.

Mr. Kirkpatrick was an organist and choir director, as well as a gospel song composer. These young Christians were holding cottage prayer meetings, and asked him for a slogan song. So he opened his heart, where sounded the abiding voice of God, and brought forth this song of redemption, grace, and glory.

The following incident reveals the high spiritual atmosphere of his life, and points out why he gave the world so many great spiritual messages that will live to bless many generations.

Mr. Kirkpatrick was in my office in Philadelphia the day the Lord called him home. "Kirk," as we familiarly called him, asked me if he could come and discuss a business matter. After a period of friendly discussion, he said, "Well, George, I'll not make a decision today; I'll go home and come back tomorrow." That night he was working on a poem in his study, where many times I had been privileged to fellowship with him. Mrs. Kirkpatrick was tired and had retired for the night. She awakened, and seeing his light, called to him, "Professor, it's very late; why don't you come to bed?" He replied, "I'm all right. I have a little work I want to finish. Go to sleep; everything is all right." Mrs. Kirkpatrick went to sleep, but when she awakened a second time and called, there was no response. Mr. Kirkpatrick had laid his head over on the chair and his spirit returned to God. My good friend had boarded

(Continued on Page 90)

SAVED TO THE UTTERMOST

"He is able also to save them to the uttermost that come unto God by Him."—HEB. 7: 25

Copyright, 1903, by W. J. Kirkpatrick. Renewal. Used by per.

W. J. K.

W. J. KIRKPATRICK

1. Saved to the ut - ter-most: I am the Lord's Je - sus, my
2. Saved to the ut - ter-most: Je - sus is near; Keep-ing me
3. Saved to the ut - ter-most: this I can say, "Once all was
4. Saved to the ut - ter-most; cheer-ful-ly sing Loud hal - le -

Sav - ior, sal - va - tion af - fords; Gives me His Spir - it, a
safe - ly, He cast - eth out fear; Trust-ing His prom - is - es,
dark - ness, but now it is day; Beau - ti - ful vis - ions of
lu - ias to Je - sus, my King; Ran-somed and par - doned, re -

wit - ness with - in, Whisp'ring of par - don, and sav - ing from sin.
now I am blest; Lean - ing up - on Him, how sweet is my rest.
glo - ry I see, Je - sus in bright-ness re - vealed un - to me."
deemed by His blood, Cleansed from un - right-eous-ness; glo - ry to God!

REFRAIN

Saved, saved, saved to the ut - ter-most, Saved, saved by pow - er di - vine;

Saved, saved, saved to the ut - ter-most: Je - sus, the Sav-iour is mine!

SAVED TO THE UTTERMOST
(Continued from Page 88)

the heavenly chariot and was off to that continuing city of which he had often written so beautifully.

The poem on which Mr. Kirkpatrick was working is a transcript of his life. It shows the source of his high spiritual conceptions which fill his compositions. Here is the poem:

> Just as Thou wilt, Lord, this is my cry,
> Just as Thou wilt, to live or die.
> I am Thy servant, Thou knowest best,
> Just as Thou wilt, Lord, labor or rest.

The second verse was written in a hurried scrawl, lacking his usual neat, firm script, showing he felt the urge to hurry, as God's call was near. Note the second verse:

> Just as Thou wilt, Lord, which shall it be?
> Life everlasting waiting for me —
> Or shall I tarry, here at Thy feet?
> Just as Thou wilt, Lord, whatever is meet.

That was all. He left this life quietly, in full obedience of a complete surrender to the will of God.

"I will receive you unto Myself, that where I am, there shall ye be also."